C000146002

www.booksbyboxer.com

Published by
Books By Boxer, Leeds, LS13 4BS UK
Books by Boxer (EU), Dublin D02 P593 IRELAND
© Books By Boxer 2021
All Rights Reserved
MADE IN MALTA
ISBN: 9781909732827

QUOTES FROM WISE CRAFT BEER ENTHUSIASTS

"THE PROBLEM WITH THE WORLD IS THAT EVERYONE IS A FEW DRINKS BEHIND."
HUMPHREY BOGART, ACTOR.

BEER FACT

THE FIRST BEER BREWERS WERE WOMEN.
BREWERIES WERE OPERATED BY
THE MOST ELITE WOMEN IN ANCIENT PERU.

A CRAFTY EXCUSE
TO HAVE A BEER

I WAS TOLD TO DRINK RESPONSIBLY,
SO I MADE SURE NOT TO SPILL ANY.

QUOTES
FROM WISE CRAFT
BEER ENTHUSIASTS

"MILK IS FOR BABIES. WHEN YOU
GROW UP YOU HAVE TO DRINK BEER."
ARNOLD SCHWARZENEGGER, ACTOR.

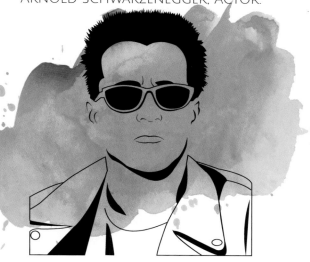

BEER FACT

THE TERM "RULE OF THUMB" ORIGINATES FROM BREWERS WHO WOULD STICK THEIR THUMB INTO THE MIX TO CHECK THE TEMPERATURE BEFORE ADDING YEAST.

A CRAFTY EXCUSE
TO HAVE A BEER

_____'S GOLDFISH DIED AND I NEEDED
TO CONSOLE HIM OVER A FEW PINTS.

QUOTES
FROM WISE CRAFT
BEER ENTHUSIASTS

"WHEN I READ ABOUT THE EVILS OF

DRINKING, I GAVE UP READING."

HENRY YOUNGMAN, COMEDIAN, MUSICIAN.

BEER FACT

Slugs and snails love the taste of beer and will leave your plants alone if you put some in your garden.

A CRAFTY EXCUSE
TO HAVE A BEER

DRINKS WERE HALF PRICE AND YOU
ALWAYS TELL ME TO BUY THE
THINGS THAT ARE ON OFFER.

QUOTES FROM WISE CRAFT BEER ENTHUSIASTS

"I HAVE TAKEN MORE OUT OF ALCOHOL THAN ALCOHOL HAS TAKEN OUT OF ME." WINSTON CHURCHILL, UK PRIME MINISTER.

BEER FACT

IN MEDIEVAL EUROPE, THE AVERAGE PERSON DRANK BETWEEN 220-250 LITRES OF BEER A YEAR!

A CRAFTY EXCUSE
TO HAVE A BEER

I ONLY DRINK BEER ON DAYS
THAT END IN Y.

QUOTES
FROM WISE CRAFT
BEER ENTHUSIASTS

"BEER, IT'S THE BEST DAMN
DRINK IN THE WORLD."
JACK NICHOLSON, ACTOR.

BEER FACT

SINCE CRAFT BEER HAS HIGH LEVELS
OF SILICON, IT'S GOOD FOR YOUR BONES.

A CRAFTY EXCUSE TO HAVE A BEER

I HEARD THERE'S GOING TO BE A DRAUGHT SO I THOUGHT I'D SAVE WATER.

QUOTES FROM WISE CRAFT BEER ENTHUSIASTS

"FILLED WITH MINGLED CREAM AND AMBER, I WILL DRAIN THAT GLASS AGAIN. SUCH HILARIOUS VISIONS CLAMBER THROUGH THE CHAMBER OF MY BRAIN — QUAINTEST THOUGHTS — QUEEREST FANCIES COME TO LIFE AND FADE AWAY: WHAT CARE I HOW TIME ADVANCES? I AM DRINKING ALE TODAY."

EDGAR ALLAN POE, POET.

BEER FACT

THE WORLD'S OLDEST DRINKABLE BEER
WAS FOUND ON A BALTIC SEA
SHIPWRECK IN 2010. THE SHIP IS SAID
TO HAVE SAILED OVER 200 YEARS AGO.

A CRAFTY EXCUSE
TO HAVE A BEER

MY WATCH DIED AND I LOST TRACK OF THE TIME (AND PINTS CONSUMED).

QUOTES FROM WISE CRAFT BEER ENTHUSIASTS

"YOU'RE NOT DRUNK IF YOU CAN LIE ON THE FLOOR WITHOUT HOLDING ON."

DEAN MARTIN, SINGER, ACTOR, COMEDIAN.

BEER FACT

The Czech Republic consume on average 148.6 litres of beer per year.

A CRAFTY EXCUSE TO HAVE A BEER

IT WAS SO WINDY LAST NIGHT THAT I WAS BLOWN RIGHT THROUGH THE PUB DOORS.

QUOTES FROM WISE CRAFT BEER ENTHUSIASTS

"FOR A QUART OF ALE IS A DISH FOR A KING."
WILLIAM SHAKESPEARE, PLAYWRIGHT.

BEER FACT

IN ANCIENT EGYPT, WORKERS WHO LIVED IN GIZA OFTEN RECEIVED BEER THREE TIMES A DAY AS PAYMENT.

A CRAFTY EXCUSE
TO HAVE A BEER

IT WAS RAINING AND THE PUB WAS
THE ONLY PLACE I COULD TAKE COVER.

QUOTES FROM WISE CRAFT BEER ENTHUSIASTS

"AH, BEER. THE CAUSE OF AND THE SOLUTION TO ALL OF LIFE'S PROBLEMS."
HOMER SIMPSON, CARTOON CHARACTER

BEER FACT

GERMANY IS THE LARGEST HOP PRODUCER
IN THE WORLD.

A CRAFTY EXCUSE TO HAVE A BEER

I NEEDED THE TOILET AND THE PUB WAS THE ONLY PLACE OPEN.

QUOTES FROM WISE CRAFT BEER ENTHUSIASTS

"BEER, IF DRUNK IN MODERATION, SOFTENS THE
MPER, CHEERS THE SPIRIT, AND PROMOTES HEALTH."
THOMAS JEFFERSON, US PRESIDENT.

BEER FACT

VIKINGS BELIEVED THAT A GIANT
GOAT WOULD BE WAITING FOR
THEM WHEN THEY DIED, WHOSE
UDDERS HAD AN UNENDING
SUPPLY OF BEER.

A CRAFTY EXCUSE TO HAVE A BEER

I BOUGHT A PINT SO I COULD
SWAP MY NOTE FOR SOME CHANGE.

QUOTES
FROM WISE CRAFT
BEER ENTHUSIASTS

"YOU CAN'T BE A REAL COUNTRY UNLESS YOU HAVE
A BEER AND AN AIRLINE. IT HELPS IF YOU HAVE
SOME KIND OF A FOOTBALL TEAM, OR SOME
NUCLEAR WEAPONS, BUT AT THE VERY LEAST YOU
NEED A BEER."
FRANK ZAPPA, MUSICIAN.

BEER FACT

IN NORWEGIAN, THE WORD "HANGOVER" TRANSLATES TO "CARPENTERS IN THE HEAD".

A CRAFTY EXCUSE
TO HAVE A BEER

MY DOCTOR SAID I NEEDED
MORE FIBER IN MY DIET.

QUOTES FROM WISE CRAFT BEER ENTHUSIASTS

"A MEAL OF BREAD, CHEESE, AND BEER
CONSTITUTES THE PERFECT FOOD."
QUEEN ELIZABETH I, QUEEN OF ENGLAND.

BEER FACT

BEER MAKES A GREAT CONDITIONER.
GOOD QUALITY BREWS APPARENTLY
GIVE YOU SOFT AND SILKY LOCKS.

A CRAFTY EXCUSE
TO HAVE A BEER

MY SATNAV LED ME TO THE
PUB AND TOLD ME I'D REACHED
MY DESTINATION.

QUOTES FROM WISE CRAFT BEER ENTHUSIASTS

"HE IS A WISE MAN WHO INVENTED BEER."

PLATO, ANCIENT GREEK PHILOSOPHER.

BEER FACT

Bruce Dickinson
(Iron Maiden frontman),
Barack Obama (former US President),
and Wil Wheaton (Actor) are
just a few celebrity
craft beer brewers.

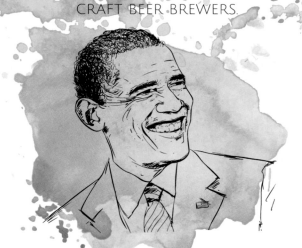

A CRAFTY EXCUSE
TO HAVE A BEER

THE BEST BEFORE END DATE IS
TODAY AND IT'D BE A WASTE NOT
TO DRINK IT.

QUOTES FROM WISE CRAFT BEER ENTHUSIASTS

"GOOD PEOPLE DRINK GOOD BEER."

HUNTER S THOMPSON, JOURNALIST, AUTHOR.

BEER FACT

'SNAKE VENOM' IS NAMED THE
STRONGEST BEER IN THE WORLD
WITH A MASSIVE 67.5% ALCOHOL VOLUME.

A CRAFTY EXCUSE
TO HAVE A BEER

NEEDED TO MAKE MORE ROOM IN
THE FRIDGE (FOR MORE BEER).

QUOTES FROM WISE CRAFT BEER ENTHUSIASTS

"BEAUTY IS IN THE EYE OF THE BEER HOLDER"

KINKY FRIEDMAN, MUSICIAN.

BEER FACT

IN SOME LUCKY COUNTRIES SUCH
AS SOUTH KOREA, PORTUGAL, GERMANY
AND FRANCE, YOU CAN ORDER
A BEER AT MCDONALDS!

A CRAFTY EXCUSE
TO HAVE A BEER

MY FOOTIE TEAM LOST AND I NEEDED
TO DROWN MY SORROWS.

QUOTES FROM WISE CRAFT BEER ENTHUSIASTS

"24 HOURS IN A DAY, 24 BEERS IN A CASE.
COINCIDENCE?"
STEVEN WRIGHT, STAND-UP COMEDIAN.

BEER FACT

A BEER'S COLOUR IS DIRECTLY RELATED TO IT'S MALT CONTENT

A CRAFTY EXCUSE TO HAVE A BEER

A LEPRECHAUN MADE ME DO IT.

QUOTES
FROM WISE CRAFT
BEER ENTHUSIASTS

"A MAN WHO LIES ABOUT BEER MAKES ENEMIES."
STEPHEN KING, AUTHOR.

BEER FACT

LEGEND HAS IT THAT BARREL-AGED BEERS WERE CREATED ACCIDENTALLY WHEN A DISTILLERY TRIED TO INVENT A WISKEY TOPPED WITH ALE FLAVOURING.

A CRAFTY EXCUSE TO HAVE A BEER

I WAS HAVING A GOOD DAY AND WANTED TO MAKE IT EVEN BETTER (CAN BE EXCHANGED FOR I WAS HAVING A BAD DAY AND WANTED TO MAKE IT BETTER.)

QUOTES FROM WISE CRAFT BEER ENTHUSIASTS

"BEER'S INTELLECTUAL. WHAT A SHAME
SO MANY IDIOTS DRINK IT".
RAY BRADBURY, AUTHOR.

BEER FACT

THE FROSTIER YOUR GLASS, THE MORE FROTH YOU GET ON TOP OF YOUR BEER.

A CRAFTY EXCUSE
TO HAVE A BEER

I THOUGHT IT WAS MY BIRTHDAY...
AGAIN.

QUOTES
FROM WISE CRAFT
BEER ENTHUSIASTS

"BEER MAY NOT SOLVE YOUR PROBLEMS,

BUT NEITHER WILL WATER OR MILK."

JOHN WAYNE, ACTOR.

BEER FACT

MORE THAN 100 MEDICINAL USES
FOR BEER HAVE BEEN FOUND IN
AUTHENTIC ANCIENT EGYPTIAN TEXTS.

A CRAFTY EXCUSE TO HAVE A BEER

ALCOHOL GEL KILLS GERMS, SO I RECKONED A PINT OR TWO WOULD DO ME SOME GOOD.

QUOTES
FROM WISE CRAFT
BEER ENTHUSIASTS

"ON VICTORY, YOU DESERVE BEER, IN DEFEAT, YOU NEED IT."
NAPOLEON, FRENCH MILITARY LEADER.

BEER FACT

IN 1814, 1.4 MILLION LITRES (AROUND 3,500 BARRELS WORTH) OF BEER SPILLED INTO THE STREETS OF LONDON AS A HUGE VAT OF BEER RUPTURED.

A CRAFTY EXCUSE TO HAVE A BEER

I SMASHED OUR PINT GLASS AND NEEDED TO PINCH ANOTHER FROM THE PUB.

QUOTES
FROM WISE CRAFT
BEER ENTHUSIASTS

"EVERYBODY HAS TO BELIEVE IN SOMETHING....I
BELIEVE I'LL HAVE ANOTHER DRINK."
W.C. FIELDS, COMEDIAN, ACTOR.

BEER FACT

BEER WAS SEEN AS CLEANER AND SAFER
TO DRINK THAN WATER DURING
THE MEDIEVAL PERIOD, DUE TO THE
FERMENTATION PROCESS.

A CRAFTY EXCUSE
TO HAVE A BEER

IT WAS _____'S LAST DAY AT WORK...
TWO MONTHS AGO.

QUOTES
FROM WISE CRAFT
BEER ENTHUSIASTS

"GIVE MY PEOPLE PLENTY OF BEER, GOOD BEER
AND CHEAP BEER, AND YOU WILL HAVE
NO REVOLUTION AMONG THEM."
QUEEN VICTORIA, QUEEN OF ENGLAND.

BEER FACT

IN 2007, A 37 YEAR OLD SCOTSMAN FROM GLASGOW SUFFERED A HANGOVER THAT LASTED FOR 4 WEEKS AFTER DRINKING JUST OVER 28 LITRES OF BEER, MAKING THIS THE LONGEST HANGOVER EVER RECORDED.

A CRAFTY EXCUSE TO HAVE A BEER

I WAS TOLD NOT TO KEEP THINGS BOTTLED UP, SO I DRANK THE BEER OUT OF THEM.

QUOTES FROM WISE CRAFT BEER ENTHUSIASTS

"I DRINK WHEN I HAVE OCCASION, AND SOMETIMES WHEN I HAVE NO OCCASION." MIGUEL DE CERVANTES, SPANISH WRITER.

BEER FACT

Cenosillicaphobia is the fear of an empty glass.

A CRAFTY EXCUSE TO HAVE A BEER

I HAVE A FEAR OF EMPTY GLASSES...

QUOTES
FROM WISE CRAFT
BEER ENTHUSIASTS

"I FEAR THE MAN WHO DRINKS WATER AND SO
REMEMBERS THIS MORNING WHAT
THE REST OF US SAID LAST NIGHT."
BENJAMIN FRANKLIN, FOUNDING FATHER
OF THE UNITED STATES.

BEER FACT

THE EARLIEST KNOWN BUILDING ON THE SITE OF DOWNING STREET IN LONDON WAS A BREWERY OWNED BY THE ABBEY OF ABINGDON, WHICH DATES BACK TO THE MIDDLE AGES.

A CRAFTY EXCUSE TO HAVE A BEER

MY OPTICIAN SAID I NEEDED GLASSES (OF BEER)

QUOTES FROM WISE CRAFT BEER ENTHUSIASTS

"I FEEL SORRY FOR PEOPLE WHO DON'T DRINK.
WHEN THEY WAKE UP IN THE MORNING, THAT'S
AS GOOD AS THEY'RE GOING TO FEEL ALL DAY."
FRANK SINATRA, SINGER & ACTOR.

BEER FACT

IN THE 1980'S, A BEER-DRINKING GOAT
WAS ELECTED MAYOR OF A TOWN IN
TEXAS AFTER THE TOWNSFOLK
BECAME FRUSTRATED WITH
CORRUPT POLITICIANS.

A CRAFTY EXCUSE TO HAVE A BEER

THERE WAS A HOSTAGE SITUATION IN THE PUB SO I COULDN'T LEAVE.

QUOTES
FROM WISE CRAFT
BEER ENTHUSIASTS

"WHISKEY'S TOO TOUGH, CHAMPAGNE COSTS
TOO MUCH, VODKA PUTS MY MOUTH IN GEAR.
I HOPE THIS REFRAIN, WILL HELP ME EXPLAIN, AS A
MATTER OF FACT, I LIKE BEER."
TOM T. HALL, MUSICIAN.

BEER FACT

PHYSICIST NEILS BOHR HAD A
PIPE WHICH CARRIED BEER
DIRECTLY INTO HIS HOUSE,
WHICH THE BREWERY CARLSBERG
PROVIDED AS AN APPRECIATION
GIFT IN 1922.

A CRAFTY EXCUSE
TO HAVE A BEER

I RAN OUT OF TEABAGS.

QUOTES FROM WISE CRAFT BEER ENTHUSIASTS

"WHOEVER DRINKS BEER, HE IS QUICK TO SLEEP;

WHOEVER SLEEPS LONG, DOES NOT SIN;

WHOEVER DOES NOT SIN, ENTERS HEAVEN!

THUS, LET US DRINK BEER!"

MARTIN LUTHER, THEOLOGIST.

BEER FACT

WHEN PRESIDENT FRANKLIN D. ROOSEVELT ENDED THE PROHIBITION IN AMERICA, HIS EXACT WORDS WERE "WHAT AMERICA NEEDS NOW IS A DRINK".

A CRAFTY EXCUSE
TO HAVE A BEER

I WANTED TO TRY MY HAND AT BEING
A PROFESSIONAL BEER TASTER.

QUOTES FROM WISE CRAFT BEER ENTHUSIASTS

"I HAVE RESPECT FOR BEER."

RUSSELL CROWE, ACTOR.

BEER FACT

IN THE 19TH CENTURY, ENGLISH BREWERS NEEDED A WAY TO EXPORT TRADITIONAL ALES TO INDIA. DUE TO THE ALES SPOILING TOO QUICKLY, EXTRA HOPS WERE ADDED. WITH THIS, INDIA PALE ALE (IPA) WAS BORN.

A CRAFTY EXCUSE
TO HAVE A BEER

I WENT TO GET A GLASS OF WATER
AND I POURED BEER BY MISTAKE.

QUOTES
FROM WISE CRAFT
BEER ENTHUSIASTS

"GOD HAS A BROWN VOICE,

AS SOFT AND FULL AS BEER,"

ANNE SEXTON, FEMINIST POET & WRITER.

BEER FACT

SOME CRAFT BEERS HAVE UNUSUAL FLAVOURS SUCH AS CHEESY PIZZA, BACON AND MAPLE SYRUP, PEANUT BUTTER, PORK, AND BANANA BREAD.

MAPLE SYRUP

VINTAGE DESIGN

A CRAFTY EXCUSE
TO HAVE A BEER

I WAS JUST ABOUT TO LEAVE
WHEN ____ CAME IN AND BOUGHT
ME A PINT.

QUOTES
FROM WISE CRAFT
BEER ENTHUSIASTS

"GIVE ME A WOMAN WHO LOVES BEER

AND I WILL CONQUER THE WORLD."

KAISER WILHELM, LAST KING OF PRUSSIA.

BEER FACT

THERE ARE ONLY TWO CATEGORIES OF BEER, ALES AND LAGERS, BUT THERE ARE OVER 100 VARIETIES BETWEEN THEM.

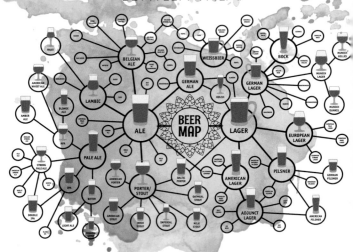

A CRAFTY EXCUSE
TO HAVE A BEER

_____ WAS HAVING 'EMOTIONAL PROBLEMS' AND NEEDED SOMEONE TO TALK TO (OVER A BEER)

QUOTES
FROM WISE CRAFT
BEER ENTHUSIASTS

"IN A STUDY, SCIENTISTS REPORT THAT DRINKING
BEER CAN BE GOOD FOR THE LIVER. I'M SORRY, DID
I SAY 'SCIENTISTS'? I MEANT IRISH PEOPLE."
TINA FEY, COMEDIAN & ACTRESS.

BEER FACT

BEER IS THE THIRD MOST POPULAR DRINK ON EARTH, AFTER WATER AND TEA.

A CRAFTY EXCUSE TO HAVE A BEER

I WAS WALKING THE DOG AND ALL OF A SUDDEN HE PULLED ME INTO THE BEER GARDEN.

www.booksbyboxer.com

QUOTES
FROM WISE CRAFT
BEER ENTHUSIASTS

"GIVE A MAN A BEER, WASTE AN HOUR. TEACH
A MAN TO BREW, AND WASTE A LIFETIME!"
BILL OWEN, ACTOR.